Alive Before You Were Born

God's Gift of Life

Written by Kim E. Bestian
Illustrated by Steliyana Doneva

CONCORDIA PUBLISHING HOUSE • SAINT LOUIS

This book is dedicated to Christ,
the life of all the living!

Published 2020 Concordia Publishing House
3558 S. Jefferson Ave., St. Louis, MO 63118-3968
1-800-325-3040 • cph.org

Text copyright © 2020 Kim E. Bestian

Scripture quotations are from the ESV Bible® (Holy Bible, English Standard Version®),
copyright © 2001 by Crossway Bibles, a publishing ministry of Good News Publishers.
Used by permission. All rights reserved.

Manufactured in St. Louis, MO/042070/416336

Introduction

What God creates is good. He is the God of life!

This book communicates the living relationship between God and every child from the moment of that child's conception. *Alive Before You Were Born* encourages spontaneous interaction between parents and children, reinforcing the truth that God made them alive from their beginning. Brothers, sisters, multiples—every child!—simply add to the family's happiness. Grown-ups are encouraged to remind growing children that life is precious and of the highest value to our heavenly Father. To Him be the glory!

As you read this book to your child, look for the heart motif in the illustrations, and ask your child to point it out to you. This is a reminder that God loves you both and sent Jesus for you. You could sing "Jesus Loves Me" or other simple songs to reinforce this message. As conversation allows, talk about the concept that you and your child were both alive before you were born and that God placed you both in your family according to His plan. End with a prayer of thanksgiving for the life He gives.

Words from God's book . . .

When God created man, He made him in the likeness of God. Male and female He created them, and He blessed them and named them Man when they were created.

GENESIS 5:1–2

For You formed my inward parts; You knitted me together in my mother's womb. I praise You, for I am fearfully and wonderfully made. Wonderful are Your works; my soul knows it very well. My frame was not hidden from You, when I was being made in secret, intricately woven in the depths of the earth. Your eyes saw my unformed substance; in Your book were written, every one of them, the days that were formed for me, when as yet there was none of them.

PSALM 139:13–16

Before I formed you in the womb I knew you, and before you were born I consecrated you.

JEREMIAH 1:5

Before you were born,
God knew you and loved you!

Before you were born,
   God sent His Son, Jesus, to save you!

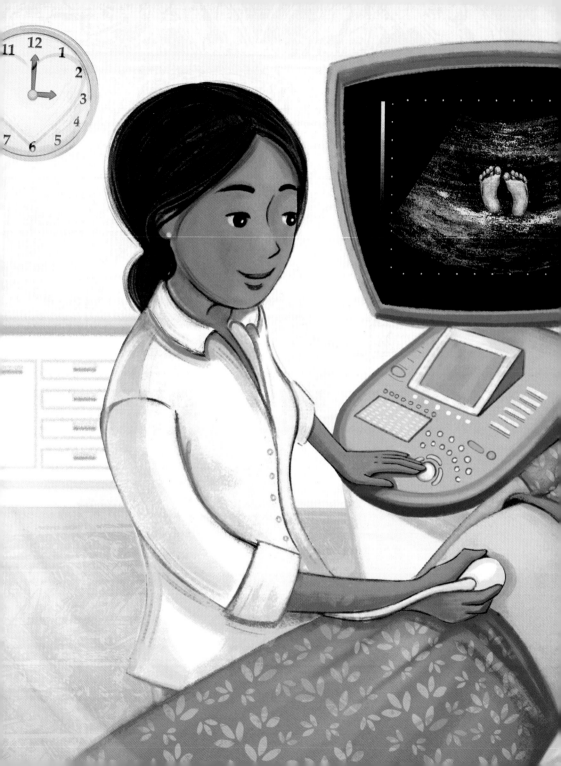

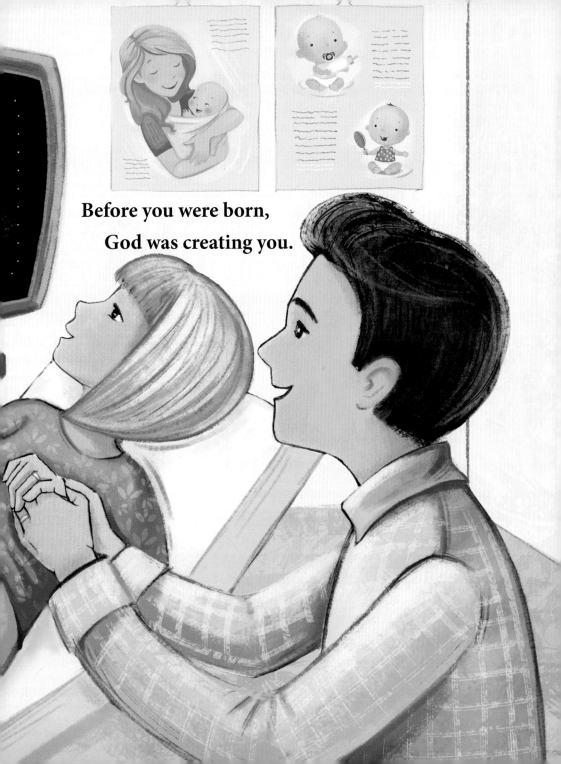

Before you were born,
God was creating you.

Before you were born,
God had a plan for your life.

Before you were born,
God formed all the parts of your body.

Before you were born,
God decided you would
be a boy or a girl.

Before you were born,
your heart was beating.

Before you were born,
God was feeding you.

Before you were born,
you took little naps.

Before you were born,
you sucked your thumb.

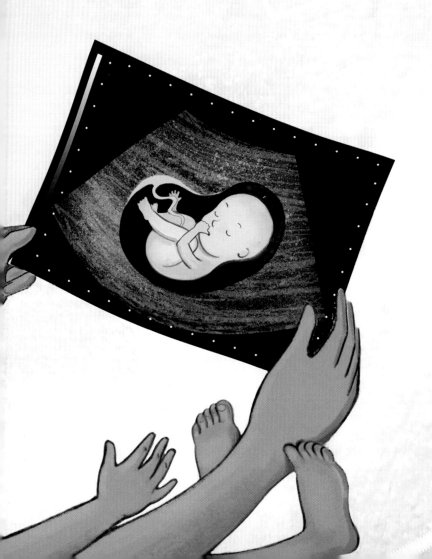

Before you were born,
you could feel pain.

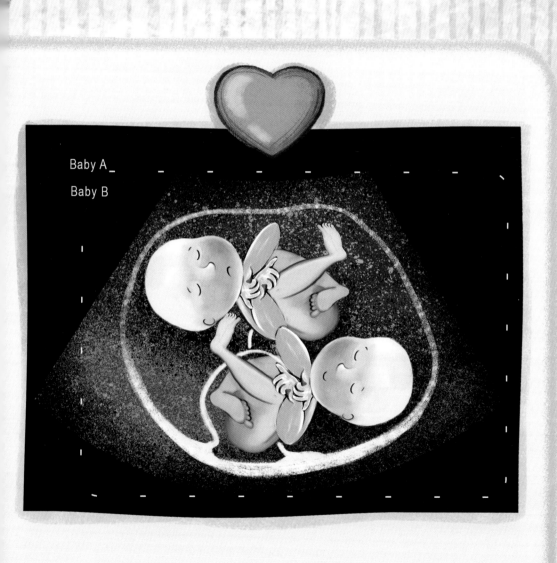

Baby A
Baby B

Before you were born,
you could move around and be happy!

Before you were born,

you kept growing all the time.

You were alive
before you were born!

That was you before you were born.

When you were born, you took your first breath of air.

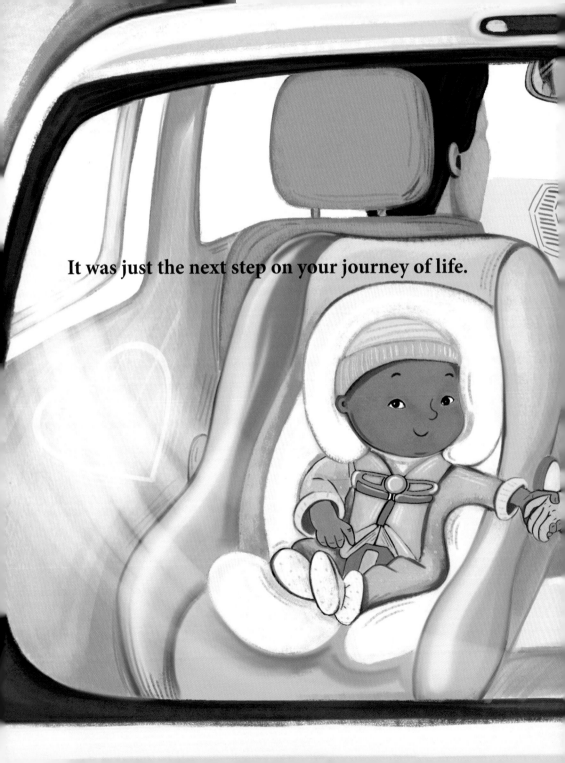

It was just the next step on your journey of life.

God knows you and loves you—always.

Praise Him!